BASS RECORDED VERSIONS

AUTHENTIC TRANSCRIPTIONS WITH NOTES & TABLATURE

Transcribed by JEFF HOLCK

The Best of POLICE

D1592957

HAL•LEONARD® CORPORATION

7777 W. BLUEMOUND RD. P.O. BOX 13819 MILWAUKEE, WI 53213

Canary In A Coalmine

By Sting

First to fall o – ver when the at - mos-phere is less than per-fect, your sen - si - bil- i - ties are
You say you want to spend the win-ter in Fi- ren - za. You're so a - fraid to catch a
Now if I tell you that you suf-fer from de-lu - sions, you pay your an - a - lyst to

sha - ken by the slight-est de - fect. }
dose of in - flu - en - za. } You live your life like a ca - nar-y in a coal mine.
reach the same con-clu - sions. }

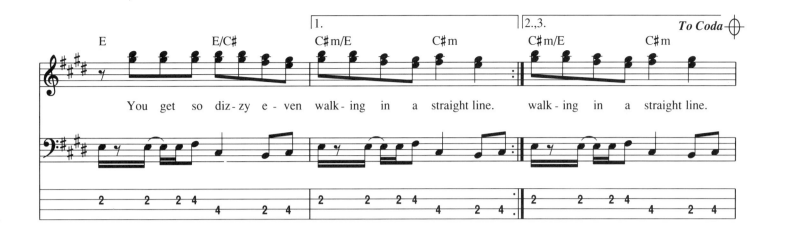

You get so diz-zy e-ven walk-ing in a straight line.   walk-ing in a straight line.

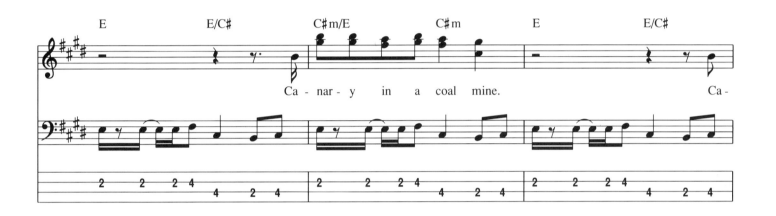

Ca - nar - y   in   a   coal mine.   Ca -

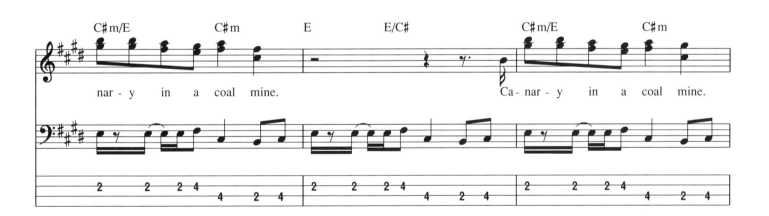

nar - y   in   a   coal mine.   Ca - nar - y   in   a   coal mine.

3

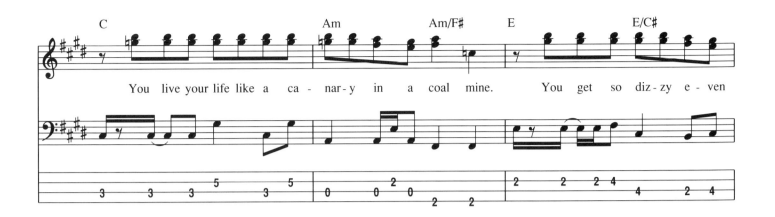

You live your life like a ca-nar-y in a coal mine. You get so diz-zy e-ven

walk-ing in a straight line. Ca-nar-y in a coal mine.

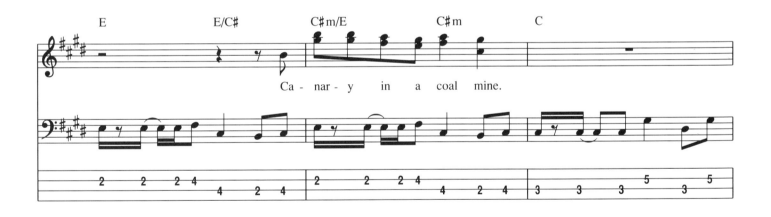

Ca-nar-y in a coal mine.

Repeat and Fade

Ca-nar-y in a coal mine.

Can't Stand Losing You

By Sting

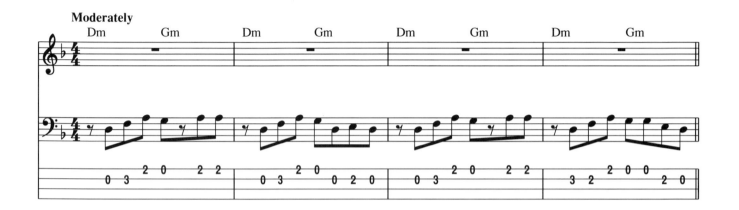

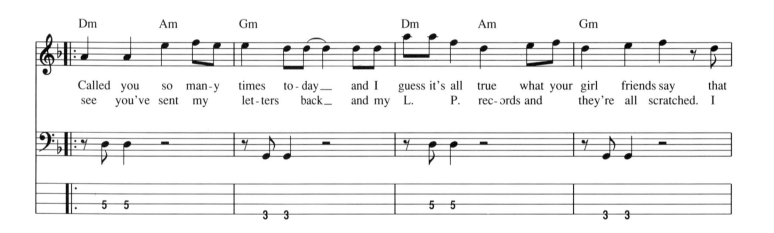

Called you so man-y times to-day__ and I guess it's all true what your girl friends say that
see you've sent my let-ters back__ and my L. P. rec-ords and they're all scratched. I

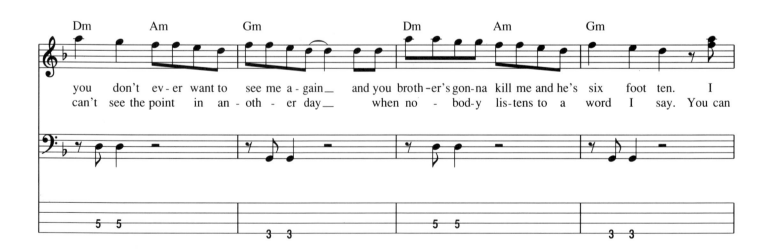

you don't ev-er want to see me a-gain__ and you broth-er's gon-na kill me and he's six foot ten. I
can't see the point in an-oth-er day__ when no-bod-y lis-tens to a word I say. You can

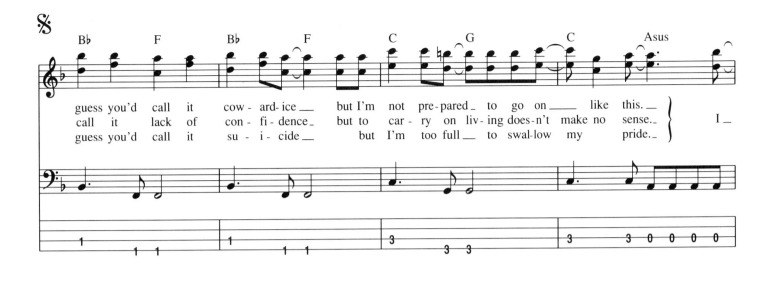

guess you'd call it cow-ard-ice ___ but I'm not pre-pared ___ to go on ___ like this. ___
call it lack of con-fi-dence ___ but to car-ry on liv-ing does-n't make no sense. ___
guess you'd call it su-i-cide ___ but I'm too full ___ to swal-low my pride. ___

I ___

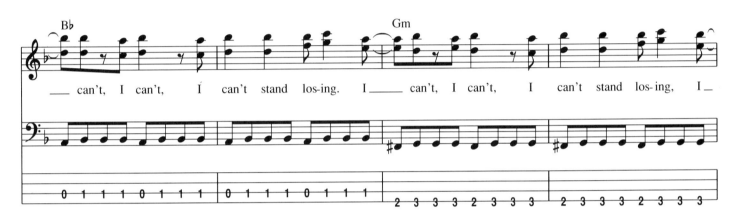

___ can't, I can't, I can't stand los-ing. I ___ can't, I can't, I can't stand los-ing, I ___

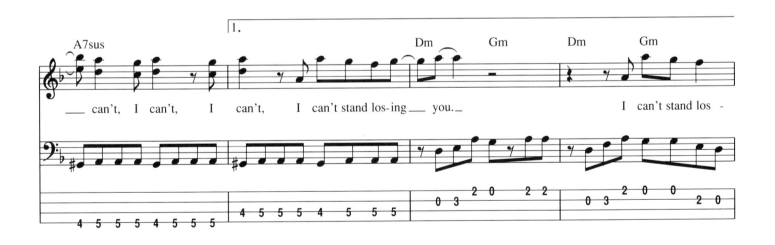

1.

___ can't, I can't, I can't, I can't stand los-ing ___ you. ___

I can't stand los -

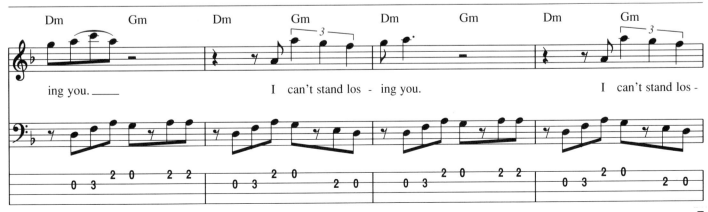

ing you. ___   I can't stand los - ing you.   I can't stand los -

De Do Do Do, De Da Da Da

By Sting

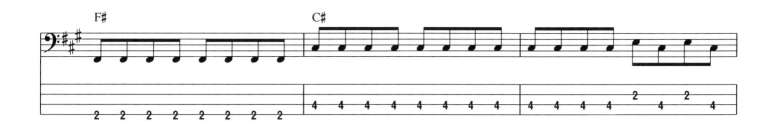

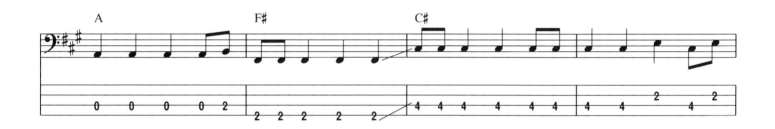

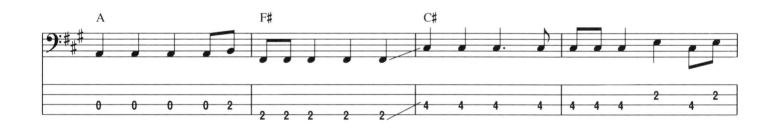

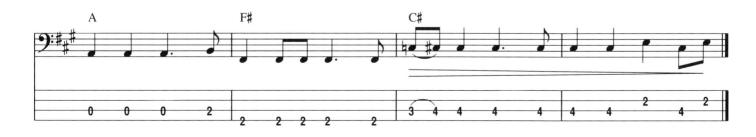

Don't Stand So Close to Me

By Sting

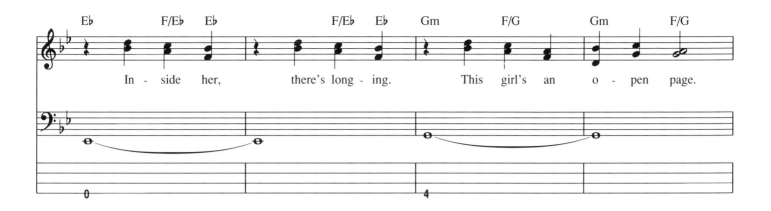

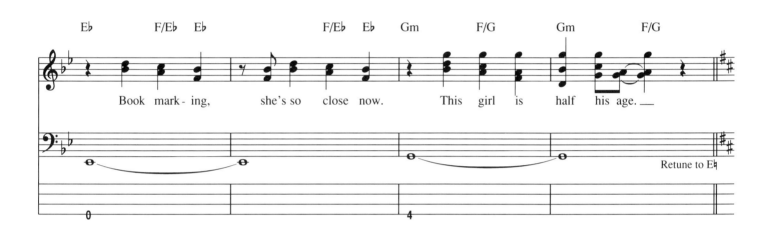

Chorus

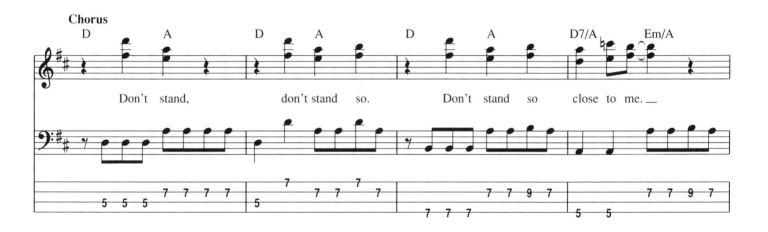

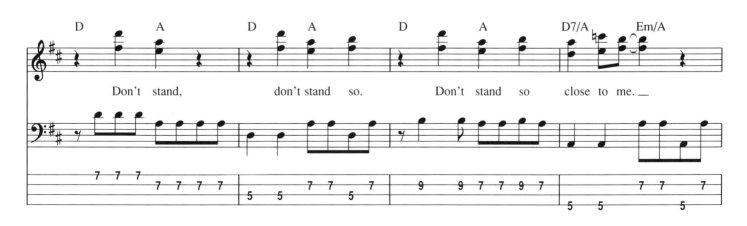

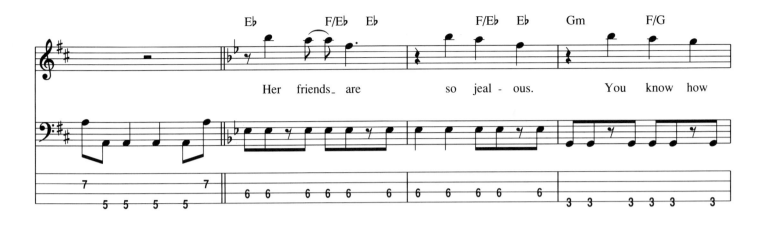

Her friends are so jeal-ous. You know how

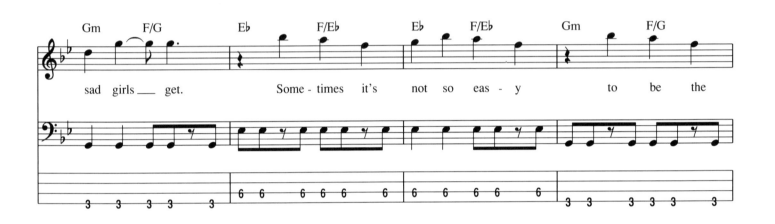

sad girls ___ get. Some-times it's not so eas-y to be the

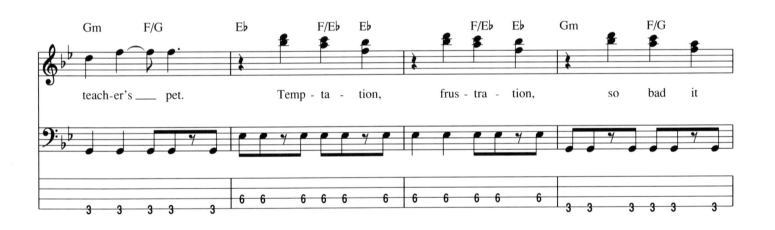

teach-er's ___ pet. Temp-ta-tion, frus-tra-tion, so bad it

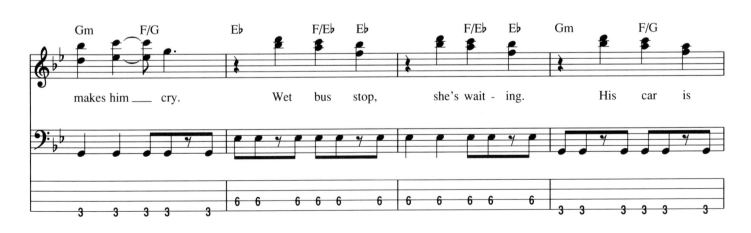

makes him ___ cry. Wet bus stop, she's wait-ing. His car is

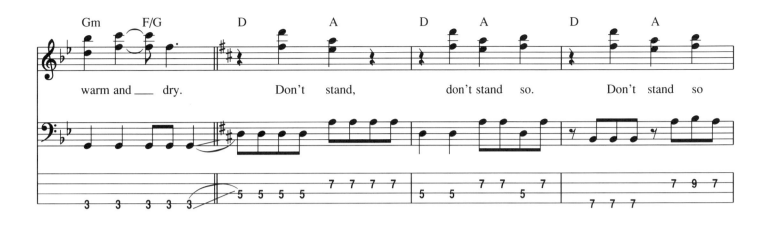

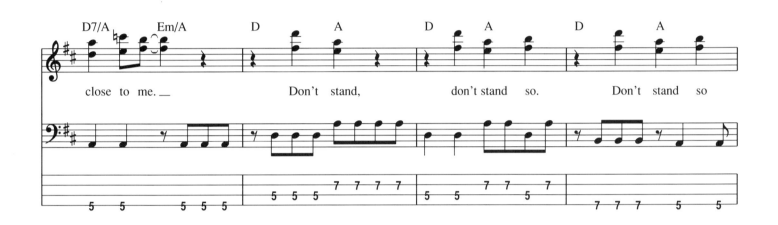

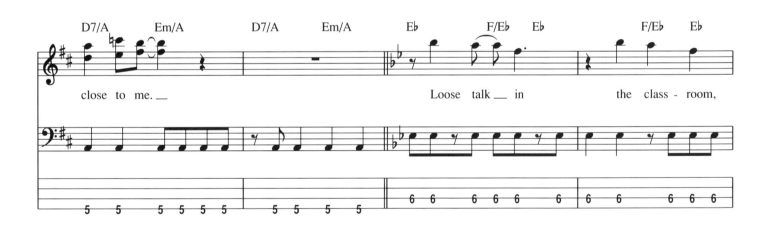

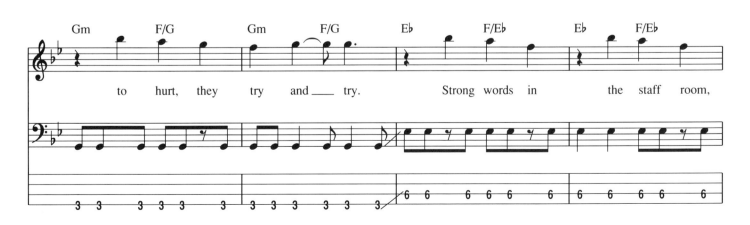

Don't stand so close to me. __

Instrumental

Don't stand, don't stand so. Don't stand so close to me. __

Bkgd. (Please don't stand so close to me.)

2nd time

Repeat and Fade

21

Born In The Fifties

By Sting

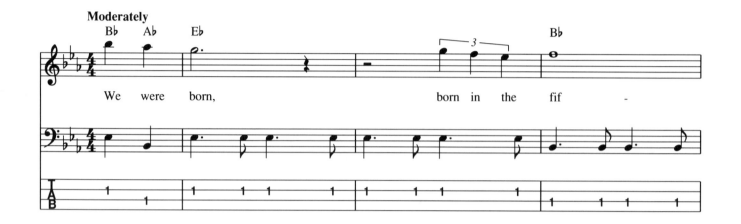

We were born, born in the fif -

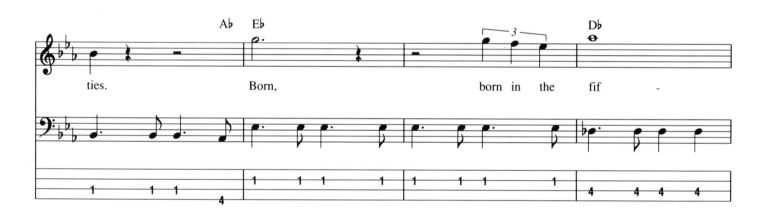

ties. Born, born in the fif -

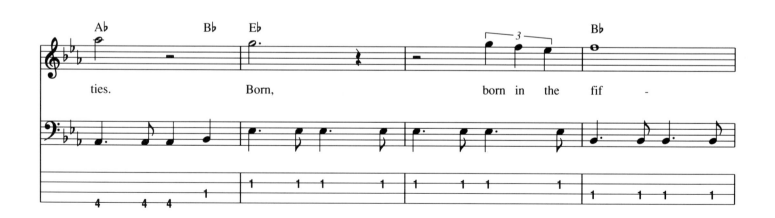

ties. Born, born in the fif -

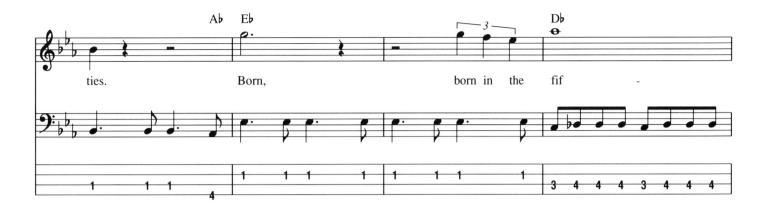

ties.   Born,   born in the fif -

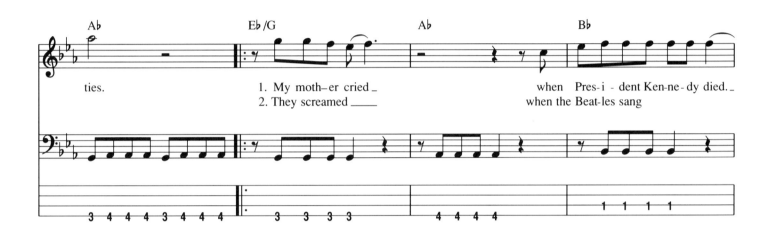

ties.   1. My moth–er cried ___   when Pres-i - dent Ken-ne - dy died. ___
                                        2. They screamed ____   when the Beat-les sang

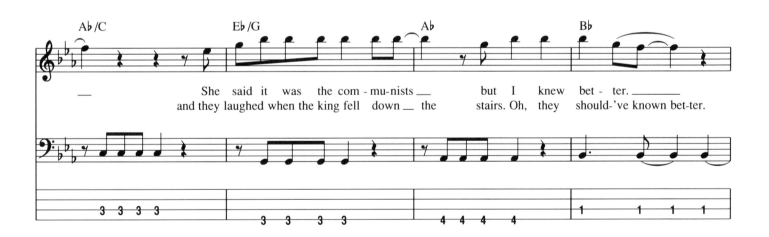

___   She said it was the com - mu-nists ___   but I   knew bet - ter. _____
                        and they laughed when the king fell down __ the   stairs. Oh, they   should-'ve known bet-ter.

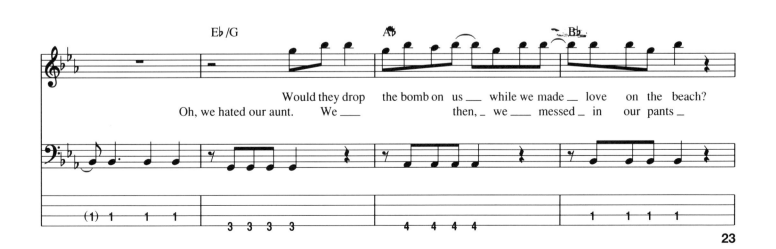

                        Would they drop   the bomb on us ___ while we made ___ love   on the beach?
Oh, we hated our aunt.   We ___   then, _ we ___ messed _ in   our pants _

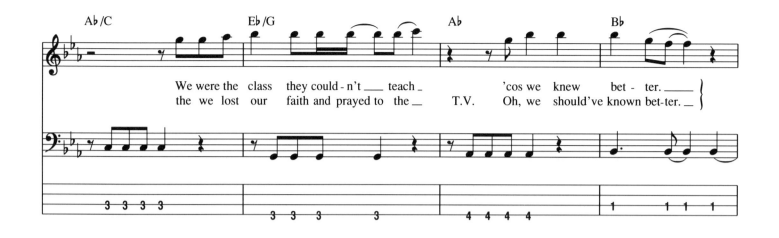

We were the class they could-n't ___ teach ___ 'cos we knew bet-ter. ____
the we lost our faith and prayed to the ___ T.V. Oh, we should've known bet-ter. __

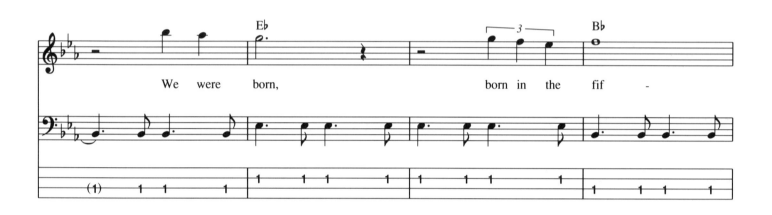

We were born, born in the fif -

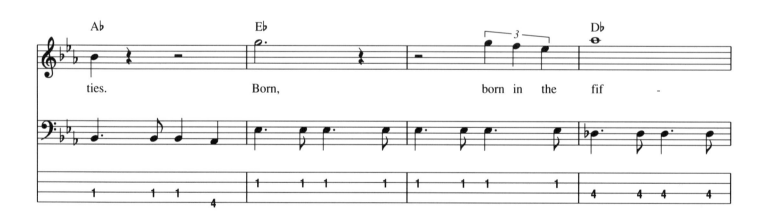

ties. Born, born in the fif -

ties. Born, born in the fif -

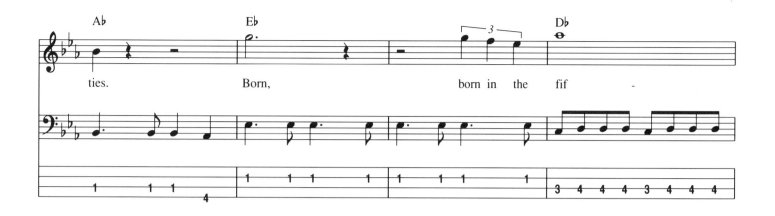

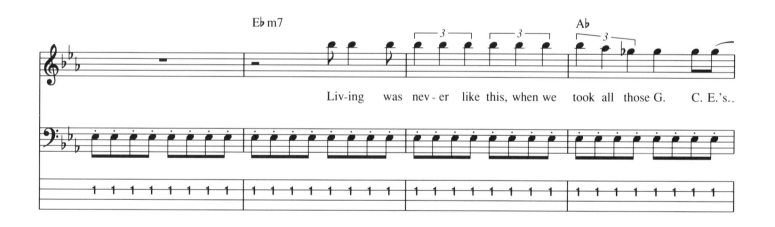

to dust. You don't _ un-der-stand us so don't rep-ri-mand us. We're tak-ing the fu-ture. We

don't need no teach-er. Born, born in the fif -

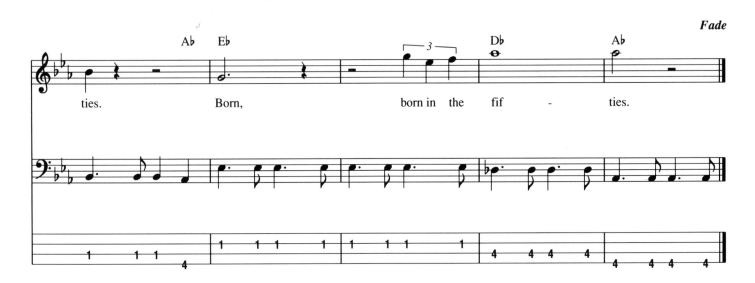

ties. Born, born in the fif - ties.

Every Breath You Take

By Sting

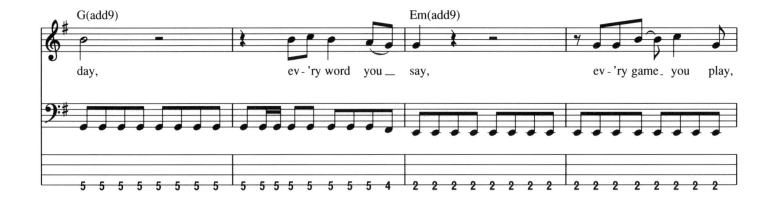

day,   ev-'ry word you __ say,   ev-'ry game __ you   play,

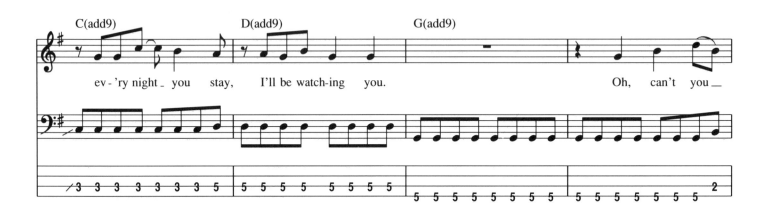

ev-'ry night __ you   stay,   I'll be watch-ing   you.   Oh,   can't you __

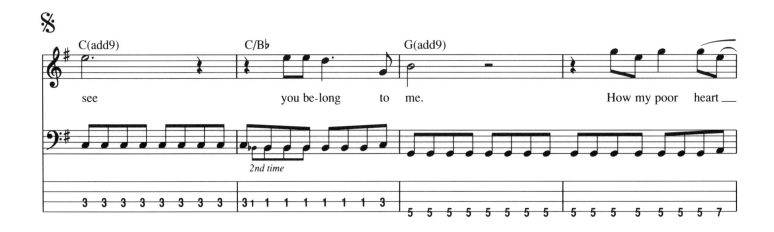

see   you be-long   to   me.   How my poor   heart __

2nd time

__ aches __   with ev-'ry step __   you take.   Ev-'ry move you __

2nd time

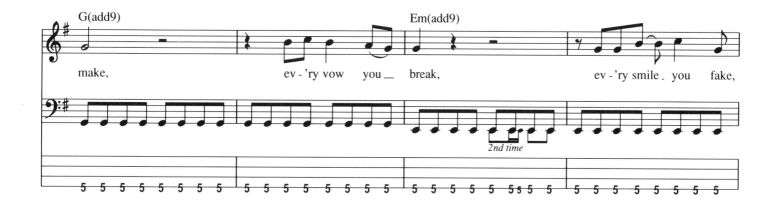

make,   ev-'ry vow you __ break,   ev-'ry smile __ you   fake,

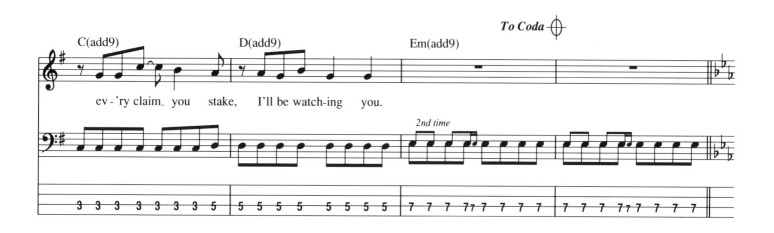

To Coda ⊕

ev-'ry claim __ you   stake,   I'll be watch-ing   you.

Since you've gone __ I been lost __ with-out __ a trace.   I dream at night. I can on - ly   see __ your face.

I look a - round but it's you I   can't __ re-place. I feel so cold   and I   long   for your __ em-brace.

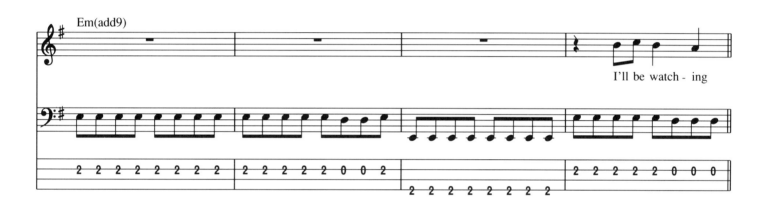

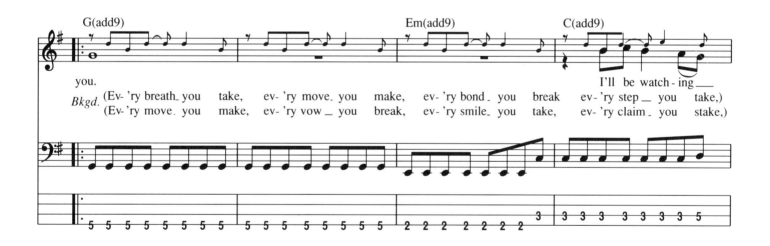

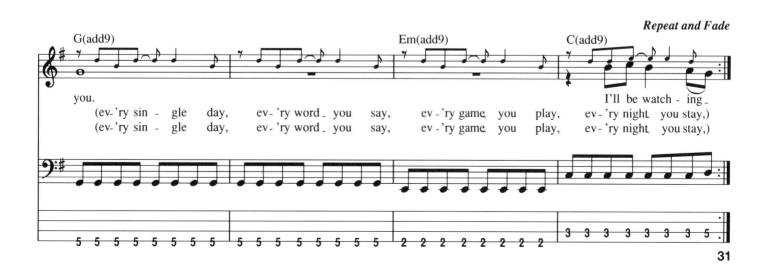

Every Little Thing She Does Is Magic

By Sting

Though I've tried be-fore_ to tell_ her of the feel-
have to tell_ the sto- ry of a thou-

- ings I have for her in_ my _____ heart, _____ ev-'ry time_
- sand rain-y days since we _ first _____ met. _____ It's a big_

_ that I _ come near_ her, I just_ lose_ my nerve_ as I've_ done from the start. _
_ e- nought um- brel- la but it's_ al- ways me_ that ends_ up get-ting wet. _

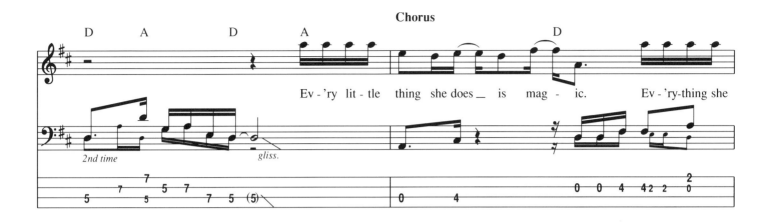

Chorus

Ev - 'ry lit - tle thing she does ___ is mag - ic. Ev - 'ry-thing she

2nd time   *gliss.*

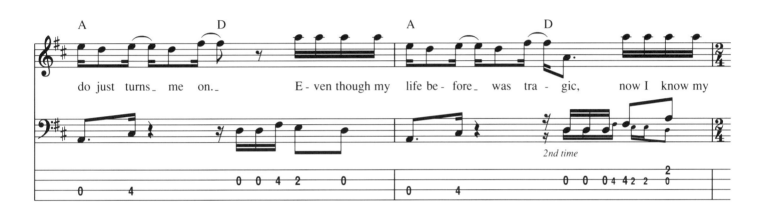

do just turns ___ me on. ___ E - ven though my life be - fore ___ was tra - gic, now I know my

2nd time

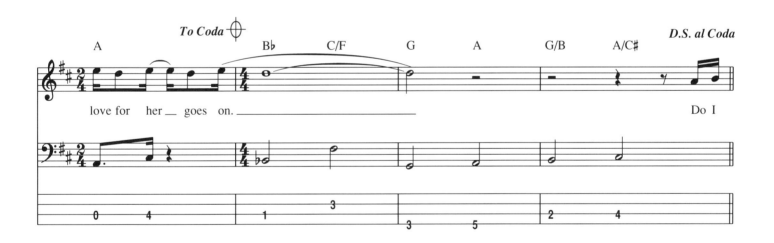

To Coda ⊕   *D.S. al Coda*

love for her ___ goes on. _____   Do I

⊕ *Coda*

I re-solved to call ___ her up   a thou-sand ___ times a day

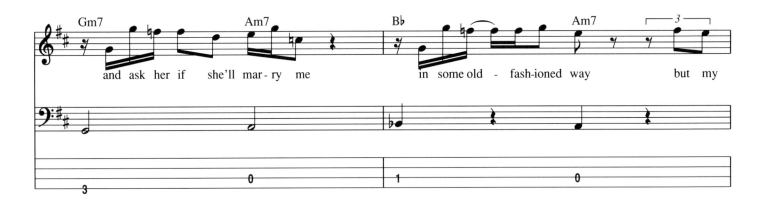

and ask her if she'll mar-ry me   in some old - fash-ioned way   but my

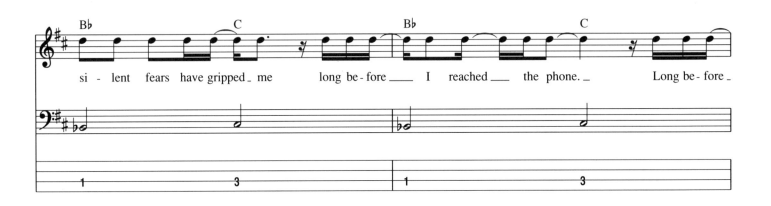

si - lent fears have gripped _ me   long be - fore ____ I reached ____ the phone. _ Long be - fore _

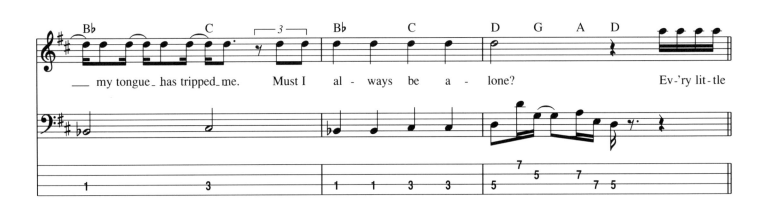

_ my tongue _ has tripped _ me. Must I al - ways be a - lone?   Ev-'ry lit - tle

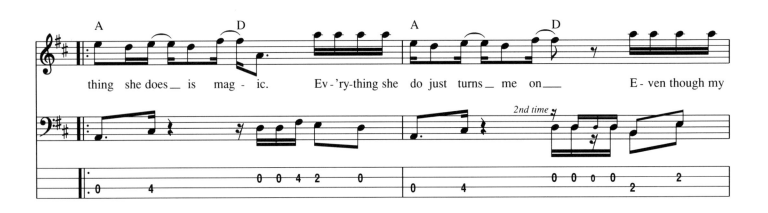

thing she does _ is mag - ic. Ev-'ry-thing she do just turns _ me on ___ E - ven though my

life be-fore_ was trag-ic, now I know my love for her_ goes on. Ev-'ry lit-tle

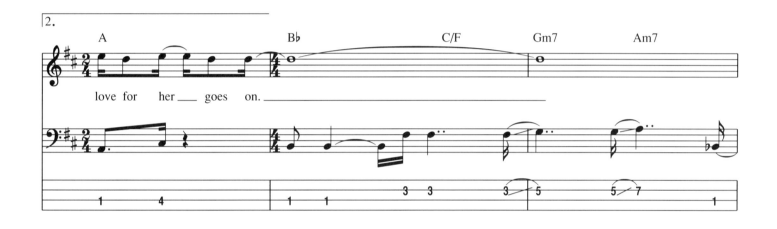

love for her __ goes on. ___

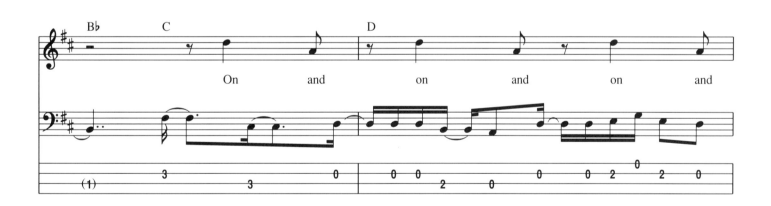

On and on and on and

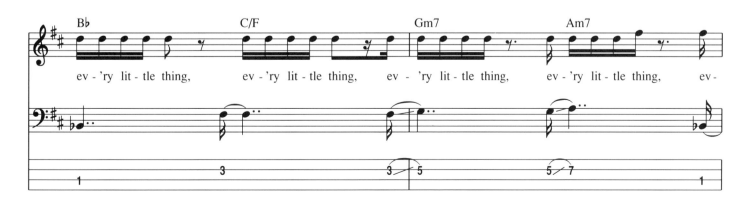

ev-'ry lit-tle thing, ev-'ry lit-tle thing, ev-'ry lit-tle thing, ev-'ry lit-tle thing, ev-

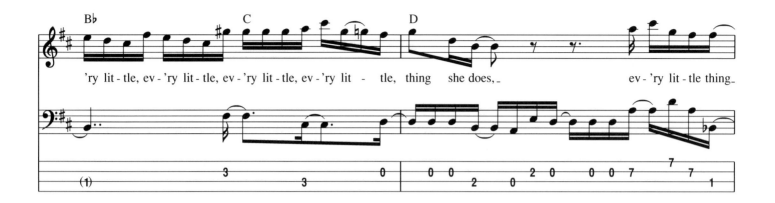

'ry lit - tle, ev - 'ry lit -tle, ev - 'ry lit -tle, ev - 'ry lit - tle, thing she does, _____ ev - 'ry lit - tle thing

_____ she does, _____ ev - 'ry lit - tle thing _____ she does, _____ ev - 'ry lit - tle thing

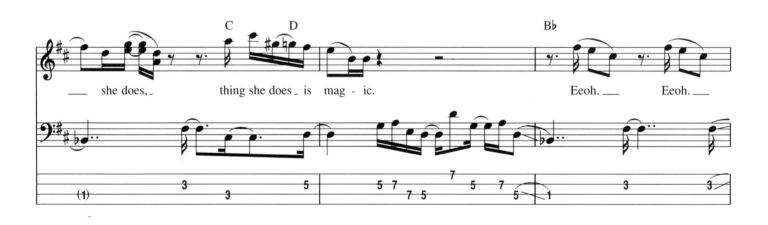

_____ she does, _ thing she does _ is mag - ic. Eeoh. _____ Eeoh. _____

Eeoh. _____ Eeoh. _____ Eeoh. _____ Eeoh. _____ Eeoh. _____ Eeoh. _____

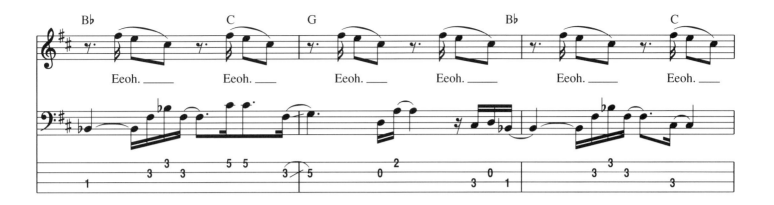

Eeoh. _____ Eeoh. _____ Eeoh. _____ Eeoh. _____ Eeoh. _____ Eeoh. _____

Eeoh. _____ Eeoh. _____ Ev-'ry lit-tle thing, ev-'ry lit-tle thing,

ev-'ry lit-tle thing she do is mag - ic, mag-ic, mag-ic, mag - ic, mag-ic, mag-ic. Oh _____

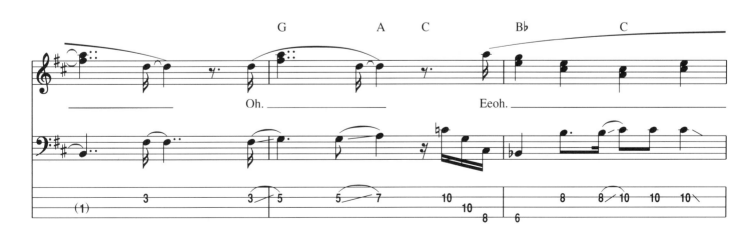

_____ Oh. _____ Eeoh. _____

Ah.

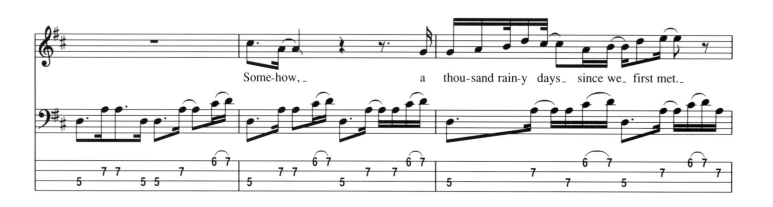

Some-how, __ a thou-sand rain-y days __ since we __ first met. __

Fade Gradually
N.C.

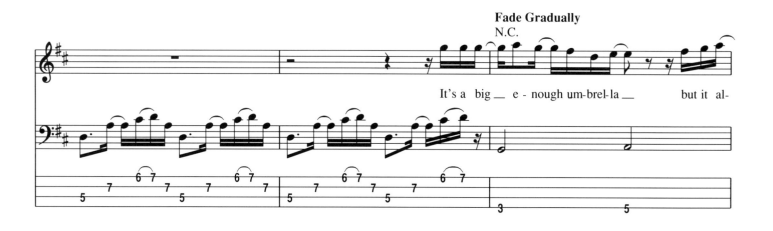

It's a big __ e - nough um-brel-la __ but it al-

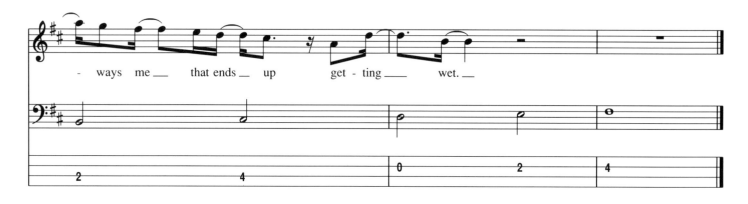

- ways me __ that ends __ up get - ting __ wet. __

King Of Pain

By Sting

flag pole rag___ and the wind___ won't stop.___ I have

Chorus

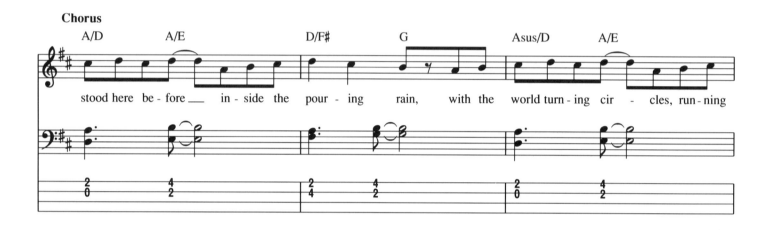

stood here be-fore___ in-side the pour-ing rain, with the world turn-ing cir - cles, run-ning

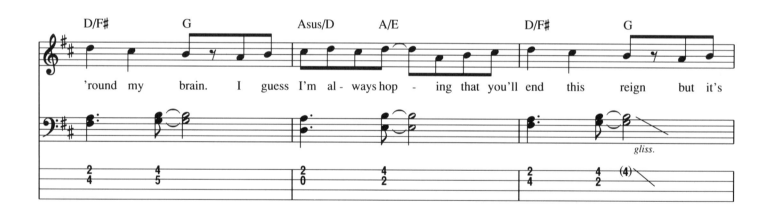

'round my brain. I guess I'm al - ways hop - ing that you'll end this reign but it's

gliss.

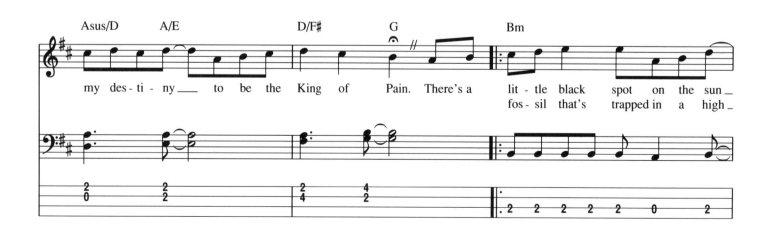

my des - ti - ny___ to be the King of Pain. There's a
lit - tle black spot on the sun___
fos - sil that's trapped in a high___

_to - day. ___ / _ cliff wall. ___   That's my soul ___ up there. ___   It's the / There's a

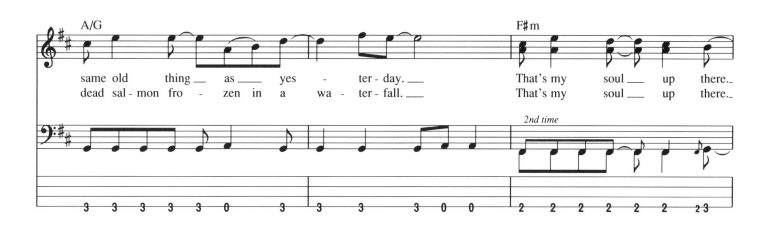

A/G   F♯m

same old thing ___ as ___ yes - ter - day. ___   That's my soul ___ up there. ___
dead sal - mon fro - zen in a wa - ter - fall. ___   That's my soul ___ up there. ___

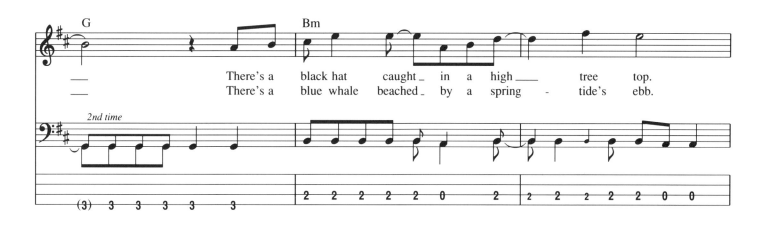

G   Bm

There's a black hat caught ___ in a high ___ tree top.
There's a blue whale beached ___ by a spring - tide's ebb.

A/G

That's my soul ___ up there. ___   There's a flag pole rag ___ and the wind ___
That's my soul ___ up there. ___   There's a but - ter - fly trapped in a spi -

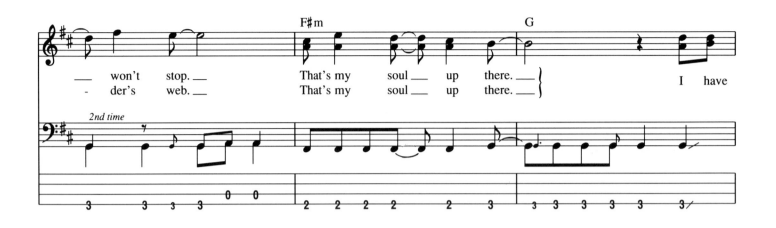

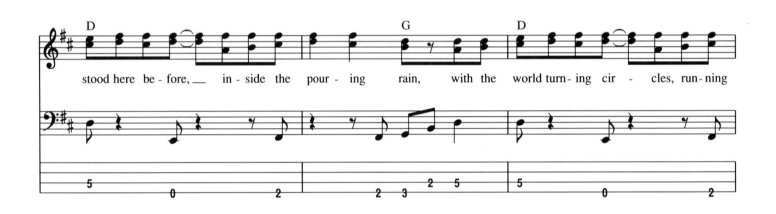

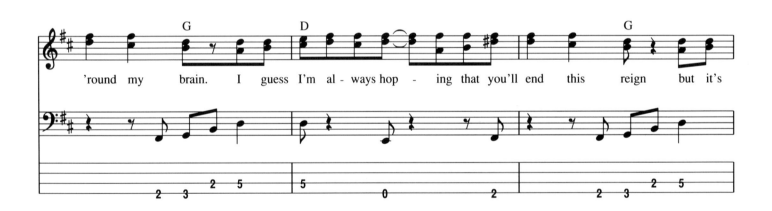

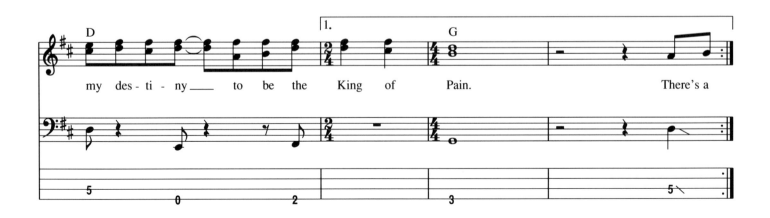

Invisible Sun

By Sting

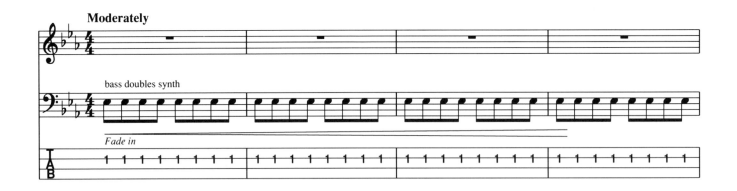

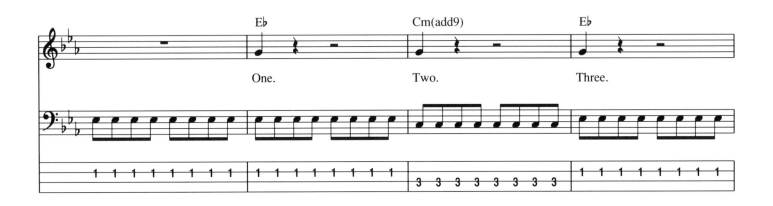

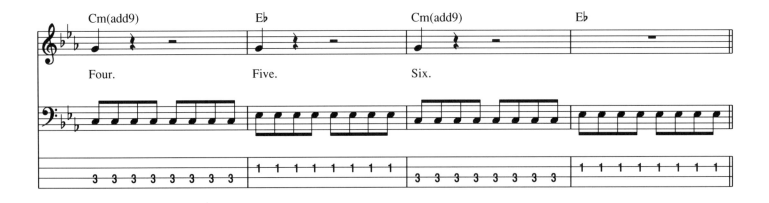

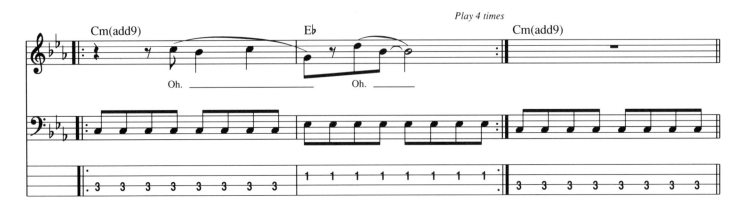

Man In A Suitcase

By Sting

Omegaman

By Andy Summers

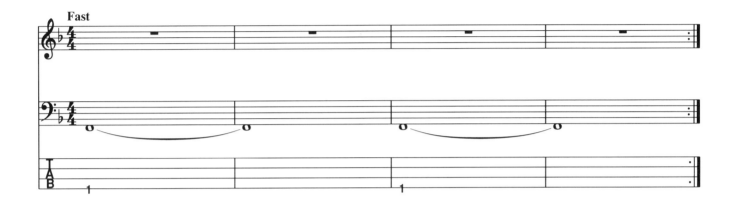

Night came down. Jun - gle sounds _____ were in _____ my ears. _____
sky's a - live with turned on ____ tel - e - vis -ion sets. _____
Time that's best is when sur - round -ings fade a - way. _____

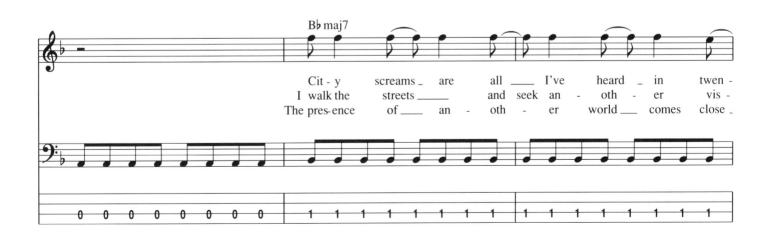

Cit - y screams _ are all ____ I've heard _ in twen -
I walk the streets _____ and seek an - oth - er vis -
The pres -ence of ____ an - oth - er world ____ comes close _

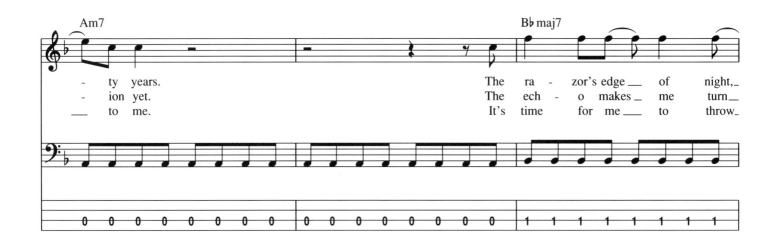

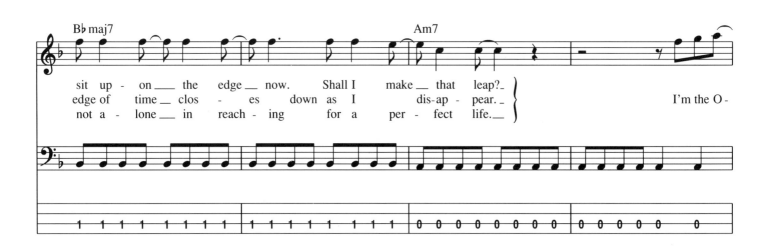

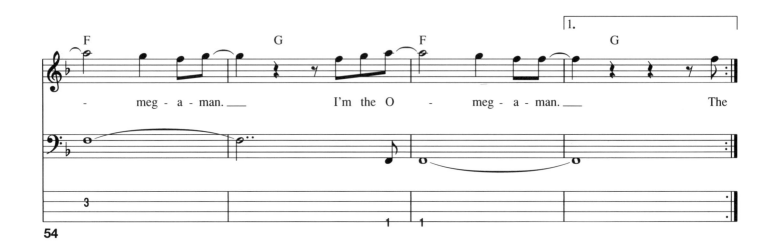

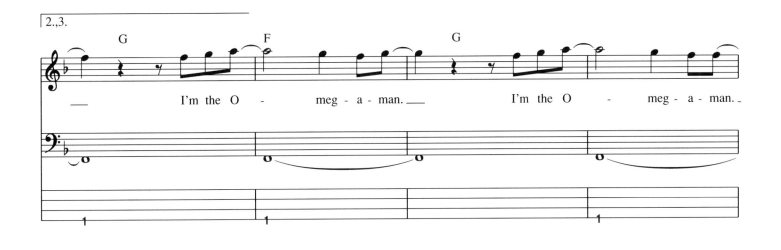

I'm the O - meg - a - man. _____ I'm the O - meg - a - man. _

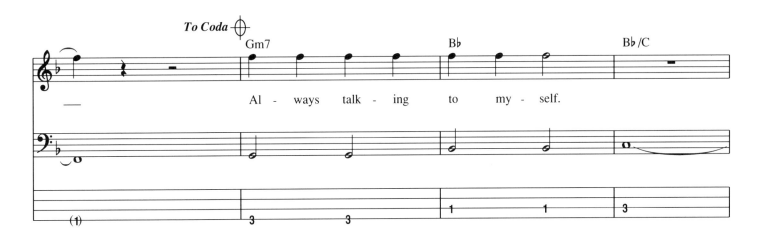

To Coda ⊕

Al - ways talk - ing to my - self.

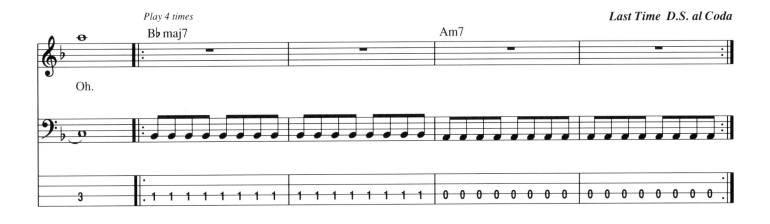

Play 4 times

Last Time D.S. al Coda

Oh.

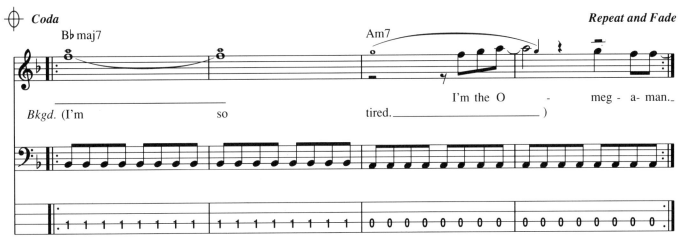

⊕ **Coda**

Repeat and Fade

Bkgd. (I'm so tired. _____)

I'm the O - meg - a - man. _

Message In A Bottle

By Sting

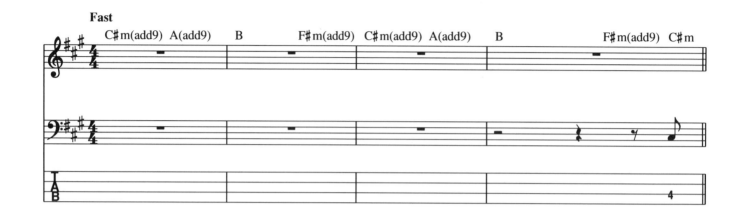

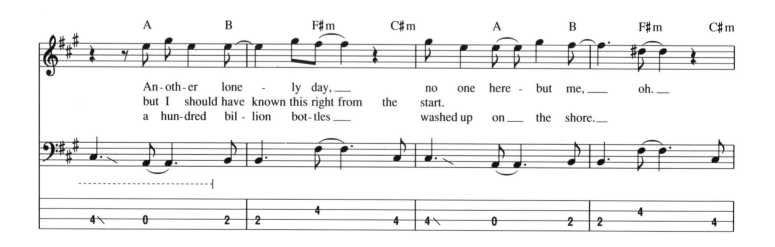

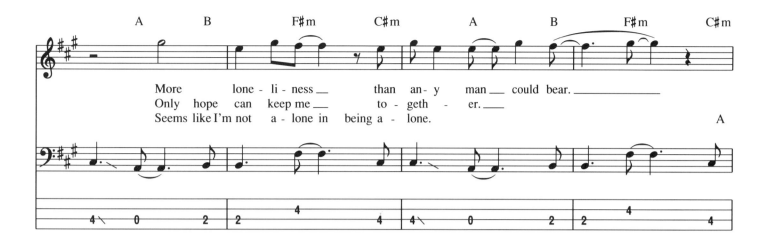

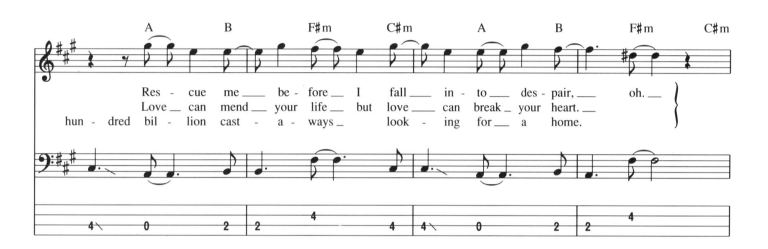

Roxanne

By Sting

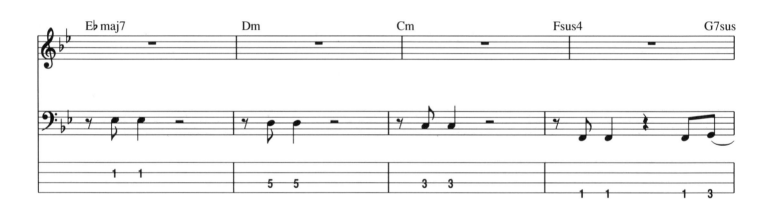

Rox - anne,
loved you since I knew you.
you ___ don't have to ___
I

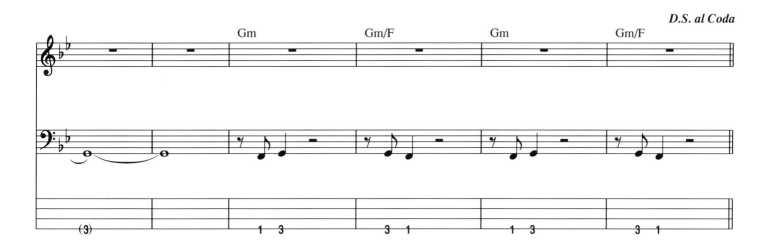

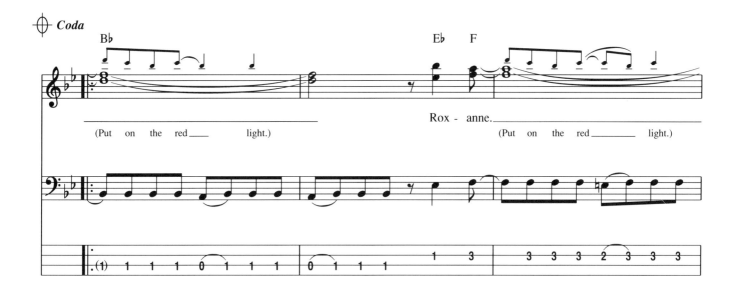

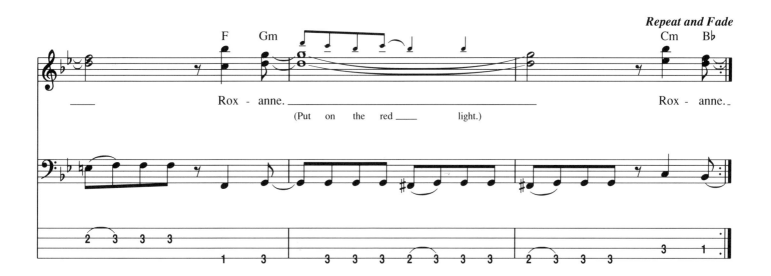

Secret Journey

By Sting

This does not seem to touch you. He point-ed to the rain.

You will see light in the dark-ness. You will make some sense of this and

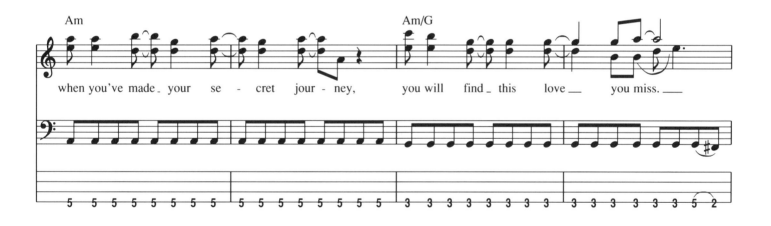

when you've made your se-cret jour-ney, you will find this love you miss.

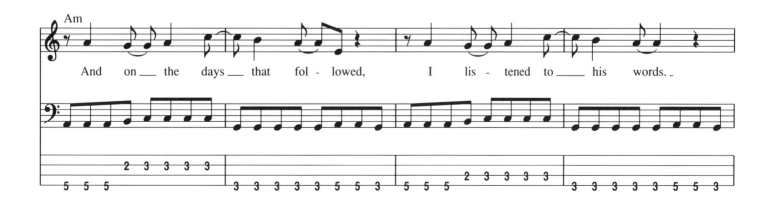

And on the days that fol-lowed, I lis-tened to his words.

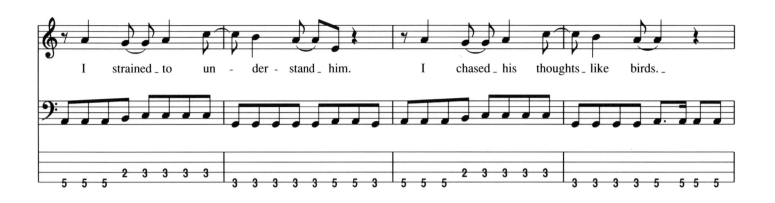

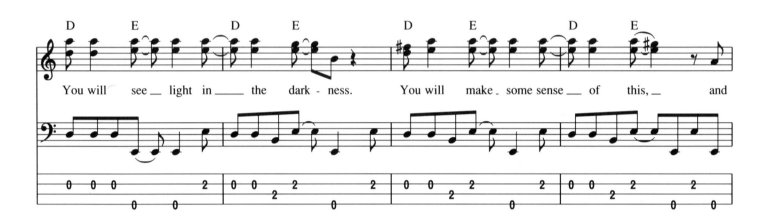

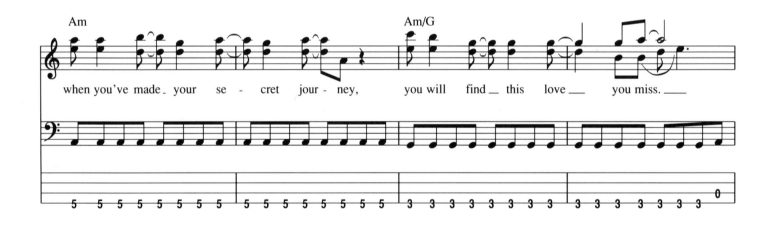

Instrumental Break

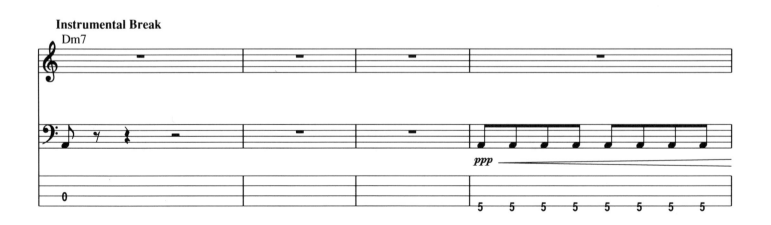

66

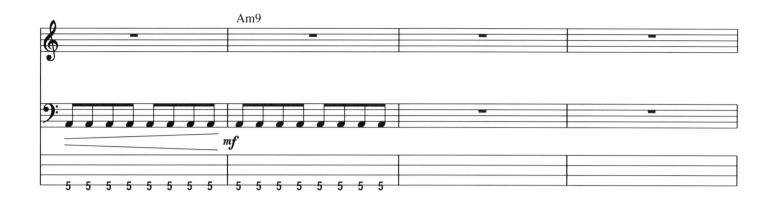

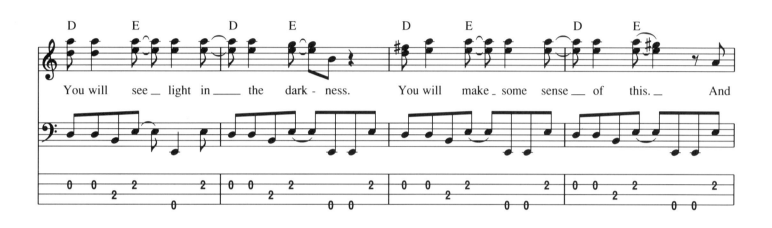

You will see light in the dark-ness. You will make some sense of this. And

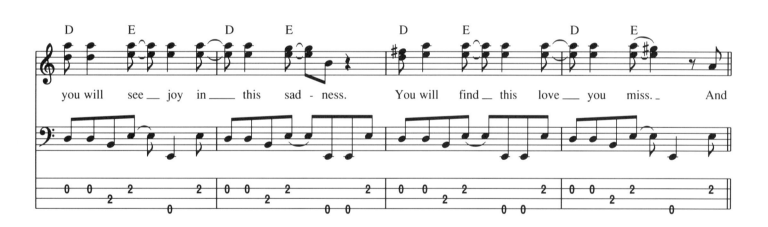

you will see joy in this sad-ness. You will find this love you miss. And

Repeat and Fade

when you've made your se-cret jour-ney, you will be a ho-ly man. And

Spirits In The Material World

By Sting

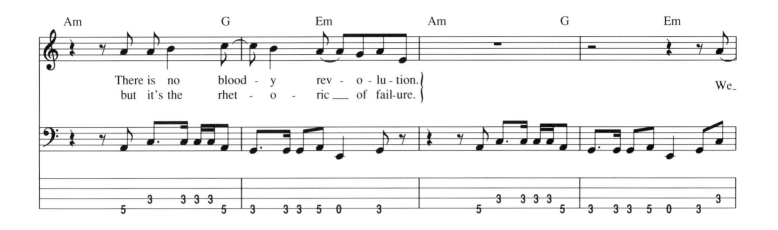

There is no blood - y rev - o - lu - tion.
but it's the rhet - o - ric ___ of fail-ure.

We_

Chorus

___ are spir-its in the ma-te - rial world, are spir-its in the ma-te - rial world,

1.

are spir-its in the ma-te - rial world, are spir-its in the ma-te - rial world.

2.

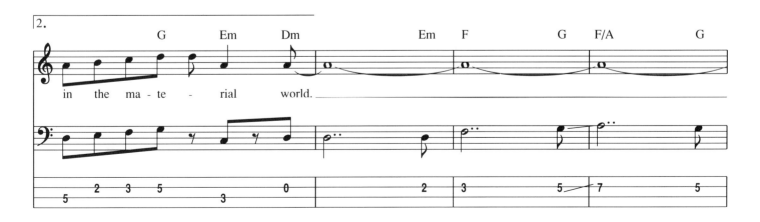

in the ma-te - rial world. _____

70

Synchronicity II

By Sting

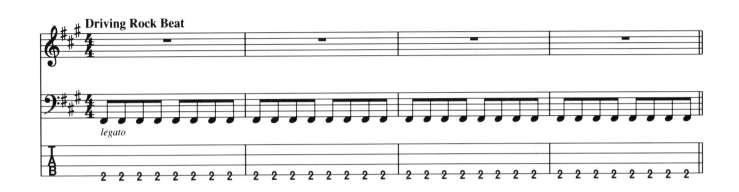

Play 3 times

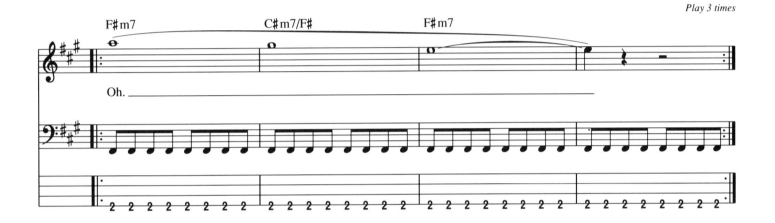

Oh. _____

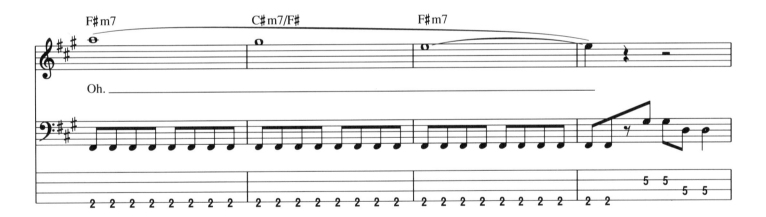

Oh. _____

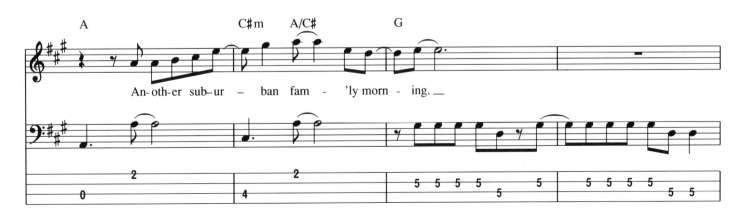

An-oth-er sub-ur — ban fam - 'ly morn - ing. ___

Walking On The Moon

By Sting

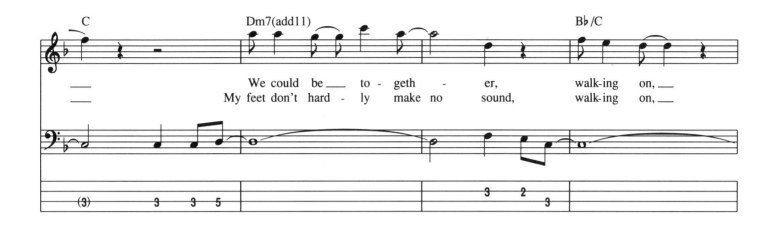

C   Dm7(add11)   Bb /C

We could be ___ to - geth - er,   walk-ing   on, ___
My feet don't hard - ly   make no   sound,   walk-ing   on, ___

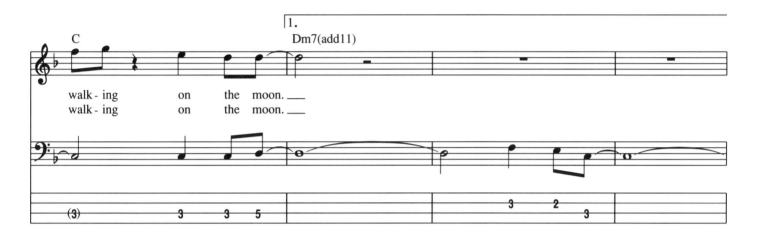

1.
C   Dm7(add11)

walk - ing   on   the   moon. ___
walk - ing   on   the   moon. ___

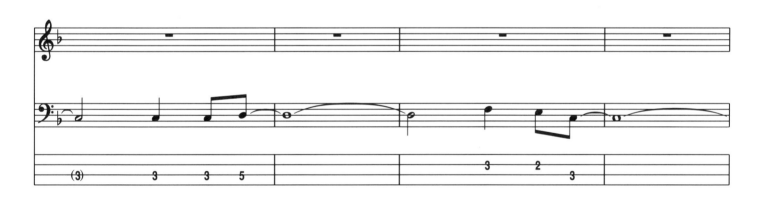

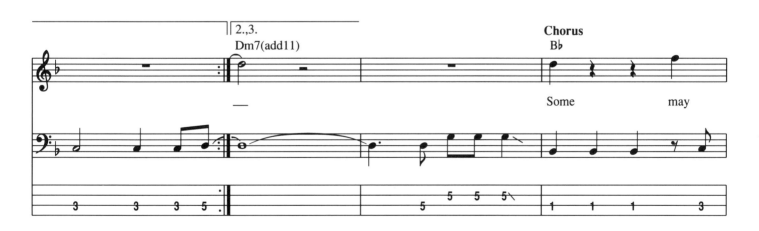

2.,3.
Dm7(add11)   **Chorus**
                                     Bb

___   Some   may

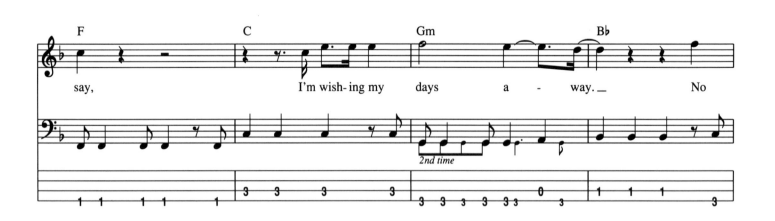

say,   I'm wish-ing my days   a - way.   No

way.   And if it's the   price   I   pay,   some

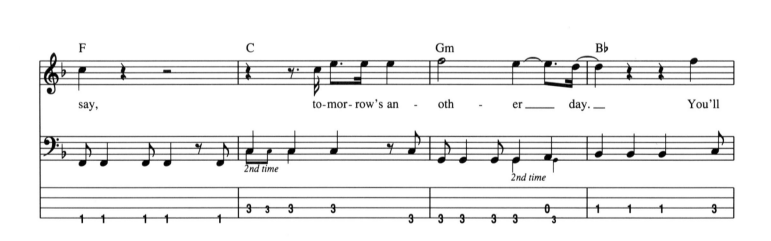

say,   to-mor-row's an - oth - er   day.   You'll

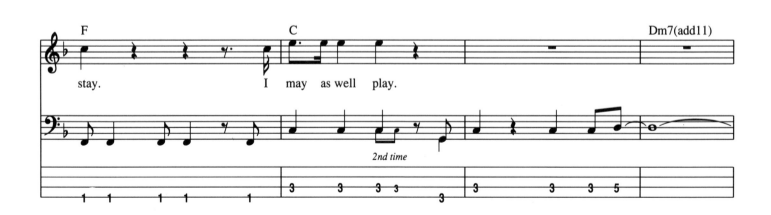

stay.   I may as well play.

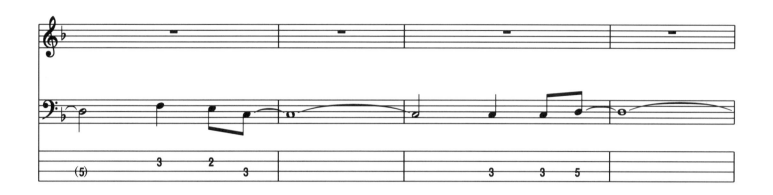

D.S. al Coda

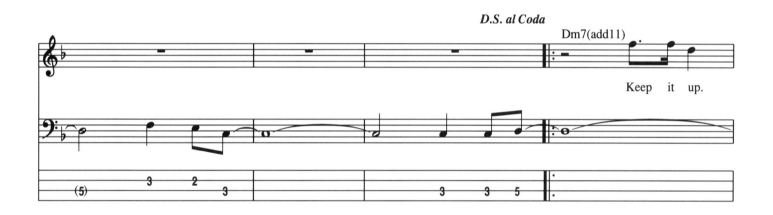

Dm7(add11)

Keep it up.

Dm7(add11)

Keep it up.

Keep it up.
Bkgd.(Ee yo.   Ee)

Repeat and Fade

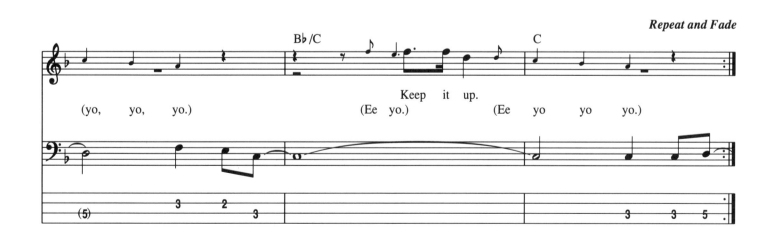

Bb /C

C

Keep it up.

(yo,   yo,   yo.)   (Ee yo.)   (Ee yo yo yo.)

Wrapped Around Your Finger

By Sting

I'll __ be __ wrapped __ a - round __ your __ fin - ger. __

Me - phis-to - phe - les __ is __ not __ your name.

I know what — you're up — to just — the same. —

I will lis - ten hard — to your — tu - i - tion. —

D.S. al Coda

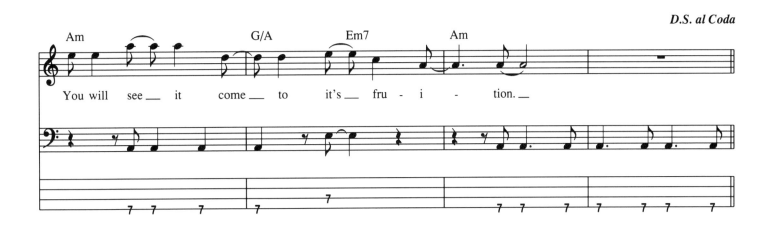

You will see — it come — to it's — fru - i - tion. —

Coda

Dev- il and — the deep — blue sea — be - hind — me. —

gliss.

When The World Is Running Down, You Make The Best Of What's Still Around

By Sting

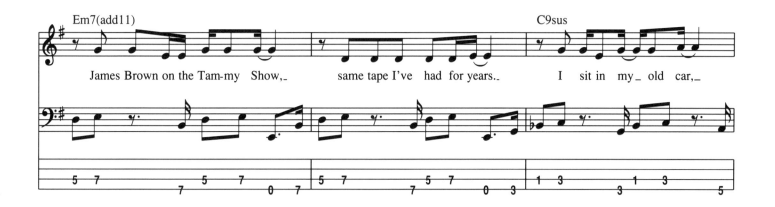

Em7(add11)

C9sus

James Brown on the Tam-my Show,_ same tape I've had for years.._ I sit in my_ old car,_

D9sus

Em7(add11)

same one I've had _ for years._ Old bat-tery's run-ning down, it ran for years and years.

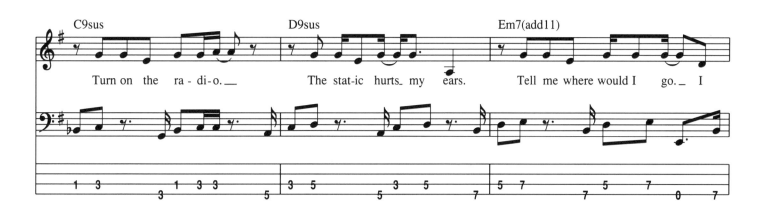

C9sus

D9sus

Em7(add11)

Turn on the ra- di-o._ The stat-ic hurts_ my ears. Tell me where would I go._ I

C9sus

D9sus

ain't been out in years. Turn on the ste-re - o._ It's played for years and years,

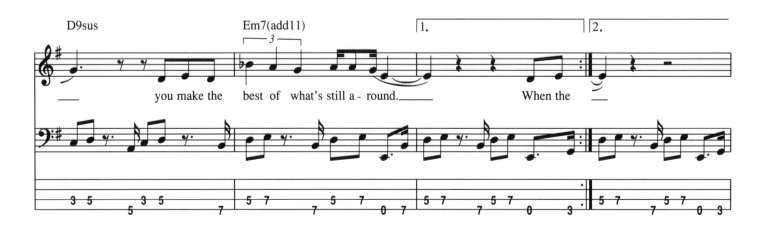

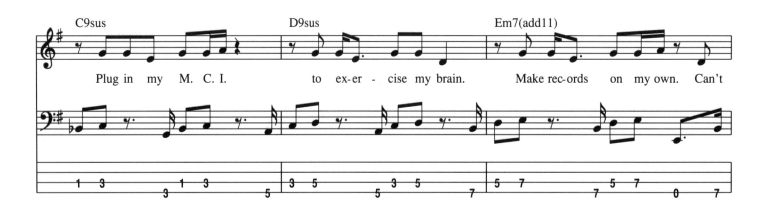

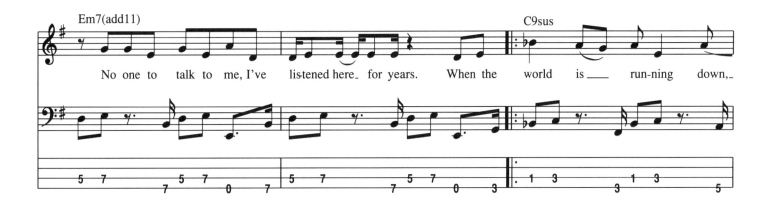

No one to talk to me, I've lis-tened here_ for years. When the world is ___ run-ning down,_

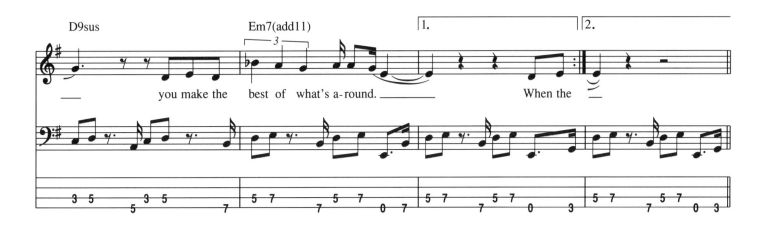

___ you make the best of what's a-round. _____ When the

Instrumental Break

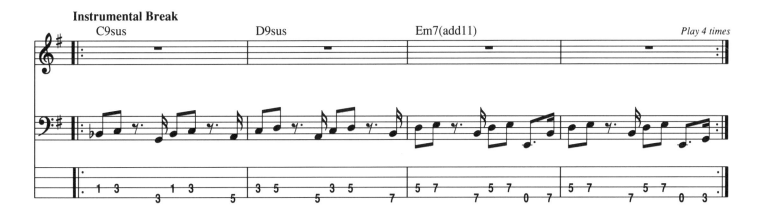

When I feel lone - ly here,_ don't waste my time with tears._ I run "Deep Throat" a-gain. It

ran for years and years. Don't like the food I eat, the cans are run-ning out.

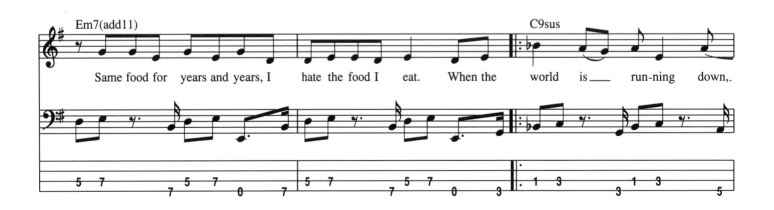

Same food for years and years, I hate the food I eat. When the world is___ run-ning down,.

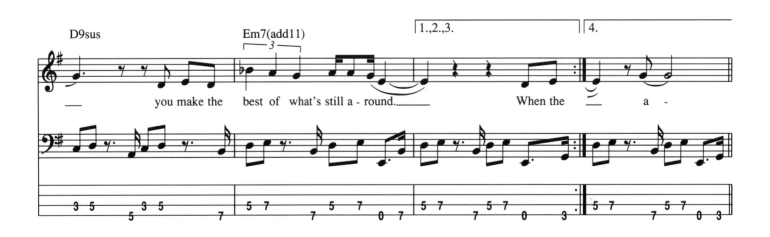

___ you make the best of what's still a - round.___ When the a -

Second time D.S. and Fade

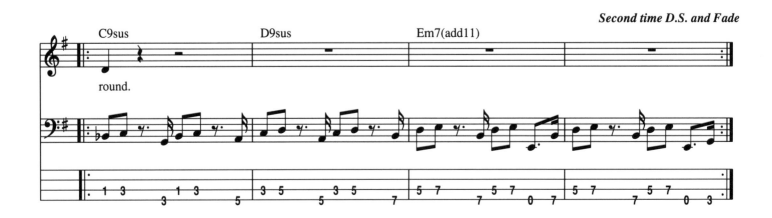

round.

BASS NOTATION LEGEND

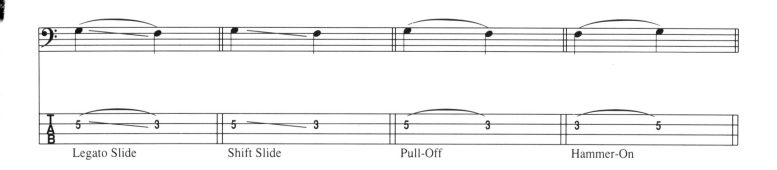

Legato Slide   Shift Slide   Pull-Off   Hammer-On

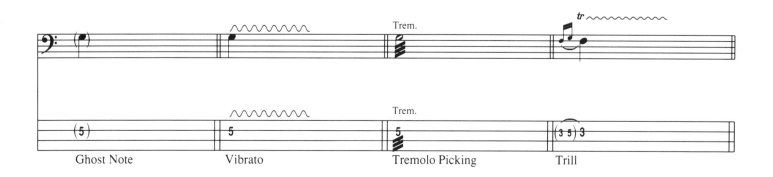

Ghost Note   Vibrato   Tremolo Picking   Trill

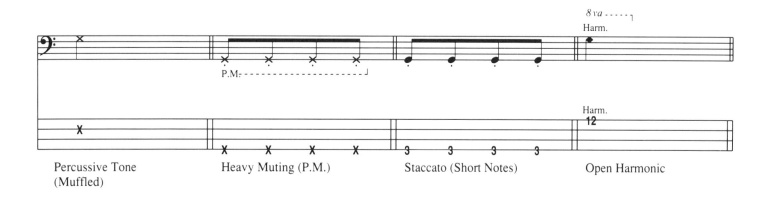

Percussive Tone (Muffled)   Heavy Muting (P.M.)   Staccato (Short Notes)   Open Harmonic

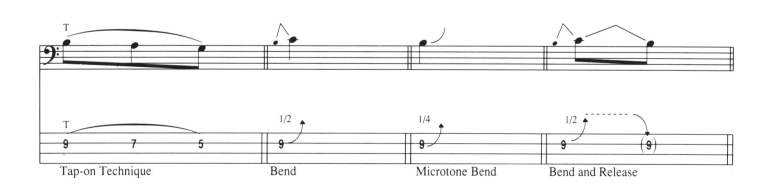

Tap-on Technique   Bend   Microtone Bend   Bend and Release

BASS RECORDED VERSIONS

Bass Recorded Versions are straight off-the-record transcriptions done expressly for bass guitar. This series features the best in bass licks from the classics to contemporary superstars. Also available are Recorded Versions for Guitar, Easy Recorded Versions and Drum Recorded Versions. Every book includes notes and tab.

Beatles Bass Book
00660103 / $14.95

Best Bass Rock Hits
00694803 / $12.95

Black Sabbath — We Sold Our Soul For Rock 'N' Roll
00660116 / $14.95

The Best of Eric Clapton
00660187 / $14.95

Stuart Hamm Bass Book
00694823 / $19.95

Jimi Hendrix — Are You Experienced?
00690371 / $14.95

Jimi Hendrix — Electric Ladyland
00690375 / $14.95

The Buddy Holly Bass Book
00660132 / $12.95

Best of Kiss
00690080 / $19.95

Michael Manring — Thonk
00694924 / $22.95

Motown Bass Classics
00690253 / $14.95

Nirvana Bass Collection
00690066 / $17.95

Pearl Jam — Ten
00694882 / $14.95

Pink Floyd — Dark Side of the Moon
00660172 / $14.95

The Best of Police
00660207 / $14.95

Queen — The Bass Collection
00690065 / $17.95

Rage Against the Machine
00690248 / $14.95

Rage Against the Machine — Evil Empire
00690249 / $14.95

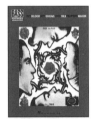

Red Hot Chili Peppers — Blood Sugar Sex Magik
00690064 / $17.95

Red Hot Chili Peppers — Californication
00690390 / $19.95

Red Hot Chili Peppers — One Hot Minute
00690091 / $18.95

Rolling Stones
00690256 / $14.95

Best of U2
00694783 / $18.95

Stevie Ray Vaughan — In Step
00694777 / $14.95

Stevie Ray Vaughan — Lightnin' Blues 1983-1987
00694778 / $19.95

FOR MORE INFORMATION, SEE YOUR LOCAL MUSIC DEALER, OR WRITE TO:

HAL•LEONARD®
CORPORATION
7777 W. BLUEMOUND RD. P.O. BOX 13819 MILWAUKEE, WI 53213

0400